Universal Justice

An emotionally-charged, full-throttle Urban Story, which dwells deep into the harsh world of drug addiction, crime and uncovers the complex lives of a money making crew seeking a better life.

A STORY OF ONE SURVIVOR

BY Carlito Kalonji Muhammad

This book is dedicated to Rodney Harris, Collins Tillman Jr. and Brother Dwayne Muhammad , May you ALL rest in Peace…I pray that Allah is Pleased with you.
To all of the suffering street soldiers…. You know who you are……. Stay strong and keep up prayer!!!!

TABLE OF CONTENTS

Thoughts from the author

I think it's extremely important that society be reminded that when it comes to the discussion of drugs and crime, the majority of Black Americans are law abiding citizens--just as the majority of Whites, Asians, Latinos, etc. are law abiding citizens.

That said, our urban Black youth are in trouble. A sizeable percentage of them have no prospect for a good education, gainful employment, societal contributions ... or even hope. Obviously, this leads to drugs, crime and punishment. One of the key problems with this phenomenon is that the criminal justice systems across the country has been functioning to warehouse these young people instead of educating, rehabilitating and preparing them for functioning within society.

I find it interesting that those folks who constantly speak about the
need for us to stop being hyphenated-Americans; conveniently
dismiss Black crime and punishment as a "Black" problem, and not
an "American" problem. So since we're on our own, I suggest to
my fellow Black men and Woman that we focus harder on keeping our young people out of the criminal justice system that we already
know is unfair, rather than focusing on how unfair the system is.

Our deepest fear is not that we are inadequate. Our deepest fear is that we are powerful beyond measure. It is our light, not our darkness, that most frightens us. Our playing small does not serve the world. We are all meant to shine as All God's children do. It's not just in some of us; it's in us all. And as we let our light shine, we unconsciously release others to do the same.

To ALL of my Brothers and Sisters seeking Righteousness. Be you Muslim,Christain,5% Nation, Freedom Fighters, Masons...let's STOP fighting amongst ourselves about the differences we have in our Beliefs...Lets' All focus on the One thing we ALL have in Common which is Satan, the Devil, Ibliss , that's in full force on us all. Especially our children. When we look into our communities we see Chaos that is not only the destruction of our communities but to our Direct Families and most of all GODS FAMILY. Drugs, crime, child abuse, spousal abuse... are all direct descendants of Greed, Envy and Jealousy. We ALL could overcome this together if we place our energies of defeating this Devil TOGETHER. When we put our energies and focus on our minor differences we allow the Devil to slip in and continue to cause havoc and mayhem. An action that he has been doing since his birth. When we come together as one Army, on the sole mission of defeating him, then he will not have a chance of survival at all. I say Stay true to your personal beliefs but Lets come together as one Army with different divisions and defeat that common enemy that we all share. The Devil. I challenge us all to unite in that one cause... Be Brave enough to accept the challenge.

Peace and Blessings
Calito Kalonji.

Universal Justice

PEOPLE, PLACES AND THINGS

Chapter 1

My name is Blue and I'm an addict. I just have a small story to share with you. An evening of a great, yet dreadful day. It all started like this….

Hey man, come on. The meeting is over already. We only got some time to get back to the house. Don't forget Madd Max is the houseman tonight and you know our ass is grass if we miss curfew. That's Q-Dog yelling at my other partner Pretty Boi.

Q-Dog is my partner I knew back when I first did time on the Island. He's from the Boogie Down. That's the Bronx NY home of the Jolly Stompers, a well known gang, down for theirs and taking everybody else's. Q-Dog just got out of drug court about 7 months ago. I met up with him in the underground ATL. Selling cds and dvds. I told him I was 30 days clean off dope and invited him to a 12 step meeting and he's been clean ever since.

Blue what's up with Pretty Boi? You know we gonna have to drag him away from the little fine shorty that was testifying her ass off tonight I replied. Yea I'm hip, but she'll have to testify for a week to shed all that behind. Both Q-Dog and Blue gave each other a strong High Five slap as they agreed on all that ass.

As our recovering family was filling out into the parking lot they finally came out. Shorty fine butt, with Pretty Boi right behind her like a little puppy begging for a bone. Wow , Q-Dog shouted. Get the girls' digits and let's be out. Pretty Boi, Madd Max is on deck tonight and I'm not going to miss curfew for you or her.

Let me tell you about Madd Max. M&M, as I call him, is 5 foot 2 inches of pure unadulterated, concentrated, recovering devil, 10 years military marine. 10 years clean off crack cocaine. By the book boss when he's on deck. Ready to chop heads off.

When Pretty Boi realized what Q-Dog had said he sprang into action like a hungry lion running down prey to feed her cubs. "Hey girl I ain't got much time. I got to get back to the spot. What's your number? 678-507-4293 rolled off her tongue as if she was thinking "Finally you asked?" That's Pretty Boi for you. The women's delight. God's gift to women. My partner. That's what I'm talking about, Q-Dog yelled. Let's bounce boyz.We out.

The three of us started our walk down 3rd st pass Miss Laura's Candy Shop. As they started walking down 3rd st it started bringing back a lot of memories. That's when Pretty Boi started talking. "You guys remember when I ran into y'all? Yeah I was having a model search, talent showcase. You pulled up in your girl's car. At that point all minds went right to that very time reminiscing…

Hey is this where Big Boi Ent is having the model

search? Yes, I said. Just stand in that line with your pictures and bio. Lil Lady will take care of you as I pointed to the prettiest Spanish mamacita produced by the Latin community. Pretty Boi looked down the line and said WOW, what are they doing giving away free concert tickets to see Jay Z? The line was about 60 deep. 40 women and 20 men. At that time he heard a voice say to everyone in line "you have to take a drug test and pass it to get down so if you know you're dirty don't waste your time or mine." When Pretty Boi heard that, he knew he wasn't going to pass. He headed straight for the front of the line. Who's in charge of the interviewing today? That would be me, I said, with Q-Dog right behind me. "Does everyone have to take a drug test today?" he asked. That's when I started explaining that Big Boi Ent was established from the efforts of two recovering addicts. That would be Q-Dog and myself. By that time I had four months clean and Q-Dog had three months. The foundation of our success was that all employees must maintain a clean and sober life during employment. At that point I looked at the line and saw forty women observing and listening to our conversation. It seemed as though they were all let down. Like they had lost their best friend or loved one. They were all fixed on Pretty Boi like one of those magnetic pieces mom always had on the refrigerators. They were all stuck on him. All Pretty Boi had to do was look at them and say "come on ladies this ain't the place for us" and believe me they would have filed out and followed him like the Pied Piper. Q-Dog saw the same thing and looked at me and said, "We gotta get him on our team."

What's your name player , I asked? Lorenzo Tipp, but

my people call me Pretty Boi. Well Pretty Boi are you going to pass the drug test? Keeping it real Pretty Boi answered, “In 3 or 4 days I could”. Blue liked that. Keeping it real from the beginning. Well if you come back to us in a week clean you would have to keep it that way to stay. Are you with that? Pretty Boi didn’t hesitate. He knew he wanted to get clean but he needed some support. Maybe this was his chance. “I’ll be back ready to go to work”. That was the start of Pretty Boi’s clean date.

Now as the three friends popped out of the reminiscing moment and back in the present time; “what time is it?” I asked. 9:30 Pretty Boi said. Man, I replied to Q-Dog. The only way we are going to get to the spot on time is to cut through the hood. We need to make this left on J Ave, “everybody down”? Without a second thought we made that left, knowing that it was the hood. The very place that was our previous stomping grounds. A one stop, cop and shop spot. Dope, girls, and trouble. Anything you wanted to get, all at one time. Not necessarily in that order. A turn that not only we should avoid but the very turn that would change each and every one of our lives. You see the twelve step program we are in taught us to stay away from old people, places, and things. I guess we thought we were special. We could do this.

As we walked further into the hood and closer to our resting spot the streets became more and more alive with the madness of organized chaos. Each person had a position to play like a well set up chess game. The first person we met was the lookouts. The lookouts job was twofold. One was to look for police, and give the signal when they were spotted.

Number two was to alert the runners when someone was pulling up trying to buy drugs. They would run to make the transaction. Shameful to say it must have been 20 runners out there. Running all over the place like a disturbed ant pile uncovered, trying to beat the next runner and make the sale. The prostitutes were about 30 deep all showing their wears and everything that came with them. The players and dealers had their cars parked on both sides of the street. The full moon that was out was complimenting the expensive paint jobs and rims each car was displaying. The only thing that overpowered the sounds of the runners and prostitutes yelling their advertisements was the 808 Base Bottom sounds of hip hop beats coming from a candy apple red, 442 heavy Chevy Chevelle, with a 411 Posey rear and a custom drop top. In fact it was Q-Dogs cousin, Top cat. Top Cat was the big baller of the hood. He supplied the entire area with work. Dope that is. There were about 5 girls dancing to the sound of the latest body grinding Hip Hop sounds out. Let me tell you, the only thing that was missing was the stripper pole strippers used to slide on. They were working what they were blessed with. Up, down, and side to side. Grinding it out.

Yo that's my cuz Cat, Q-Dog said. I'm gonna holla at him for a minute. Then he asked Pretty Boi to go into the store across the street and get a pack of cigarettes. Pretty Boi had no problem complying. He wanted to follow Nini, the neighborhood fly girl in the store anyway. Here I am in a place I don't want to be, waiting for my two best friends. As I waited for them outside the store, a young boy approached me. Hey what's up Dad? I got that hard on deck. Showing me a handful of rock cocaine. The chemical devil himself. He was no older than 16 yrs old. I'm alright Black, I told him. Well whatever you need Dad, I got it. That's ok, I'm good. If you're good then what the hell are you doing standing here. You must be the man. At that point I was on the verge of not only ready to tell the young buck what I was about but ready to show him what I was about when I heard a voice say "Hey, Hey. Chill out youngster that's Blue from 40 PJ's. He's good wherever he's at,in the hood. That was Kool Aide. We did a lot of crime work together back in the day. Yo Blue what are you doing hanging on the block? I hope you aint back on that dog food." That's the street name for heroin. I had a 10 year addiction. Had to have it. By any means possible. I kicked it going cold turkey but I needed the help of the 12 step program to stay clean. That's my support system with the help of the God of my understanding.

Naw man me and the boys just taking a shortcut through the hood on the way home. I hear that, Kool-Aide said. Well hurry up kid. This ain't the place for anybody trying to get their stuff together. I'm proud of you Blue. All of you. That's when I looked across the street and saw Cat and Q-Dog kickin it. I then looked over the mass movement and knew I had to get things moving. I went into the store to hurry Pretty Boi up.

I should have known Petty Boi had totally forgotten what he was sent in the store for. He was begging Nini for some time and she was steady teasing him. Nini was fine but she was still on that rock. People say that she was the finest thing in the hood before she got hooked. I can't imagine that a woman could be finer than that. Nina was built like a Brick House in Buckhead Ga. She had curves for days that was backed up with a healthy body for days. Any man's dream. It shows to tell you , that rock cocaine is not prejudice, to anyone, shape, color or form.

"Come on Pretty Boi" I said. "What's going on"? That's when Pretty Boi asked me to stand in the line and get the cigarettes while he walked Nini out to her car. Here we go again. I'm picking up all the pieces. Now while I was standing on the line my cell rang. It was LT. LT is the Lieutenant of the 3rd ward. He's 20 years clean off heroin. Father of three as well as a loving husband. Strong advocate of cleaning up the hood in which he came from.

What's up LT ? I said. He asked how and what I was doing? When I was answering him I heard gunshots and mass confusion outside. A common sound in the hood. At that same time LT told me to hold on. He returned back to me 30 seconds later and said he had a call coming in that he had to handle, he'd get back with me later. I then ran outside to see what was going on. That's when Nini met me crying and shouting that they just shot Q-Dog and Pretty Boi. That's when I looked up over to Top Cats car. It was shot up like it was driving down the middle of Main street in Beirut. I ran to the car and there they were. Q-Dog slumped over the drivers door, Pretty Boi lying in front of the car in a pool of blood, and Top Cat laying across the front seat as if he was trying to get a heater out of the glove compartment. My boyz was hit and I don't know what happened.

As I knelt down over Pretty Boi holding his head in the palms of both hands it seemed to me that he was the only one alive. Looking into Pretty Boi's eyes, once the eyes that would make a 25 year old virgin saving herself for her wedding night, give it up to him the day before her wedding, were now the eyes screaming for help. The look of dying. Trying to hold on to life. Slowly fading away. Not being able to talk because of a bullet wound to the neck, upper back, and upper right shoulder. Pretty Boi looked back into Blues eyes as if to say, "I had nothing to do with this but God is close so don't leave me until he comes."

At that moment Blue looked up and realized a crowd of crack heads all in Cats' car rambling for anything. Dope, crack, money, or anything they could sell. Back the fuck up Blue screamed, as he was faster that Cat was, and opened up the glove compartment, got the gun and bust about 4 shots off in the air. "Get the hell back before I put one in one of you dirty jays" Blue screamed.

What great timing Blue thought as he watched all the Js running for cover, at the same time the police were creeping in on him, guns drawn, shouting, " Put the weapon Down and put your hands in the air." Blue quickly dropped the gun thinking, Wow these cops think I'm the gunman. He was absolutely right. The police thought they had their suspect. As the crowd was screaming Blues' innocence, the police converged on Blue and tackled him to the ground anyway. With a knee in his upper back and forearm across the back of his neck, they pulled his arms behind him and put the handcuffs on him. The cuffs were so tight his hands were literally turning color. They rushed Blue into the nearest squad car and commenced to secure the crime scene.

As Blue sat in the patrol car he watched how the block transformed from the dark dreary hood into Times Square New York on New Years Eve. Lights everywhere. 20 maybe 30 patrol cars. This is the police's license to terrorize the neighborhood. They really don't care anything about the injured or possible deaths. To them it's just another black on black crime in a known drug area.

The ambulance came and took Pretty Boi and Q-Dog off to the emergency room. Top Cat died on the scene. As they were taping off the area, Blue saw LTS squad car pull up. Yes he thought. All he had to do was talk to LT and he would be let go.

As the police were pushing the onlookers back away from the crime scene Blue noticed LT getting information from his officers. Detectives were speaking to a couple of people and like always they were trying to get their 15 minutes of fame not really knowing what the hell went on. Blue saw how the officers were speaking to LT. They were giving him all the facts that they knew of the situation when they pointed to the car he was in. LT looked his way and along with one of the officers that handcuffed him, started walking his way. So many things were running through Blues head. From the first time he was in trouble with the law since age 10 to the here and now. WOW here we go he thought. In the middle of chaos that had nothing to do with him but it seemed like he knew about every detail. He knew that it wasn't going to be easy with LT. Either way it went, it wasn't going to be nice. One thing he knew for sure, he could only tell them what he knew, which was nothing. And that was the truth.

The officer with LT opened the driver door and rolled down the back window. When LT saw that it was Blue in the car he told the officer to roll up the window, close the door and come with him. LT was pissed off Blue thought, as he watched them walk back to Top Cats car.

LT spoke to everyone at the scene that may have seen what happened. After about 30 minutes LT emerged from the crowd and came back to the car Blue was in. He opened the door and told Blue to get out. Blue attempted to speak but LT stopped him and said, “All I want to know is what part you played in this mess.” Blue told LT that he had nothing to do with it and he didn’t know what the hell happened. LT and Blue got in the car and looked at the scene. What a mess.

ONE MAN ARMY

Chapter 2

Sirens blaring, women crying, home boys arguing were the immediate sounds that assaulted my ears. So many police cars with lights on looked like a combination of the lighting of the Macys Christmas Tree and the dropping of the Big Apple on New Years Eve in Nightlight everywhere. The only survivor of the Top Cat Crew (that's what the police named them) was Q-Dog. Pretty Boi died on the operating table 20 minutes after he arrived at the hospital.

The doctor told me that he was going to be o.k. In the eight days that he was in the hospital Q-Dog was going in and out of conscientiousness due to the meds he was taking. He thought that he was dying so he started admitting to me a lot of stuff. Like he stopped using drugs but he continued to help his cuz, Top Cat. Q-Dog stated that he was Top Cat's protection, and one day a rival crew was trying to take over Top Cat's drug trap.Q-Dog stopped that action quickly and the result was the ambush that got Q-Dog lying in his hospital bed. They would never come at Q-Dog straight up. A drive by is the only way they could have gotten him. The only thing is Q-Dog didn't die. As I was looking at him in that bed I noticed a tattoo on the right side of his chest. It said One Man Army. I asked him what that was all about. He told me that when he was about 14 years old he, his mom and his sister were going through a lot of changes. Q-Dog then started telling Blue how he got the name. It started one day his mother and his step dad were having one of their many fights. The whole thing started like this:

"I'm only going to ask you one more time!!!Where is my shit? That's Q-Dog's step dad, Jose talking to his mom. He's an insane Cuban refugee that doesn't take any mess from nobody. He thinks he's the owner of God's World. José married Q-Dogs mom, Sandra, when he was about 3 years old. Q-Dog's mom was in love only because she thought that she couldn't get any better. José was sort of a Don Juan look alike. A Cuban Fly Guy that could charm the rattle right off the tail of the snake itself without getting bit. He also had a flip side that would make the Devil change his own ways like he was the Virgin Mary herself. Ever since Q-Dog could remember, Jose was putting his mitts on him and his mom. He was very controlling and abusive.

I told you Jose, I don't know where it's at." Maybe you forgot where you hid it' "Sandra said. At that moment, José hit Sandra with a backhand slap to the head that could be heard clearly to China. Sandra went down hard, hitting her head on the hard kitchen floor. Being protective of his mother and sister Q-Dog jumped on Jose's back trying to choke the life out of him. Let me say that Jose was a heavy PCP user and being bigger , stronger and high off of PCP , Jose reached behind his head, grabbed Q-Dog, and slammed him right on top of Sandra ,driving his knee into his back. Putting all his weight on the both of them, he started laughing as he looked down on them. Yelling at the top of his lungs Jose screamed, “As long as I’m the big boss man in this house, don’t ever try that crap again!

I’ll be back for my stuff tonight, and if my stash ain't here , all of you better be gone too! José rose up and left saying something in Spanish, laughing.

“Are you ok baby?” Sandra asked Q-Dog. “Mom why do you let that monster keep doing what he wants to you? If you're afraid, why don’t we just get help. I hate that monster, ‘Q-Dog said with a vengeance in his voice.

Boy watch your mouth. José is a good man. “He just has a little drinking problem”.” Ma that ain’t beer. That negro is high off of PCP. One day he's gonna flip and try to kill us all if we don’t get help or kill him first. “Stop that crazy talk boy, and take that garbage out. We're gonna be ok, and you better stop that cussin". Q-Dog , mad and upset, grabbed the garbage out of the kitchen and started out of the door mumbling as he was leaving.

“What’s that Percy?” Nothing Mom!! Please call me Q-Dog. Your name is Percy, she said. That’s what I named you and that’s what I call you. If you know better , you better stop giving me all that lip. Now take that garbage out. Q-Dog went to the incinerator to dump the garbage. There was so much in the bag that he couldn’t put it all in at one time. He had to take some out piece by piece to throw it away. As he was putting the garbage into the shoot, a couple of players were going up to the roof. TNT and Spider. “What’s up, young buck? It’s good to see you helping her ma”, TNT said”. Yea that’s how we do it in the 40 PJ’s.We help each other come up”, Spider said giving Q-Dog a pat on the shoulder for encouragement. At that time Q-Dog was at the bottom of the bag as he pulled out a square brick-like package. It looked like someone had carefully wrapped it up like a present prepared to go under a Christmas tree. Spider and TNT's eyes got as big as basketballs. Like they have just seen a ghost. Hey, hey, hold on. Don't throw that in there. What is it? Both TNT and Spider said at the same time. "I don't know. I'm just throwing this stuff out for my mom". "Let us get that then". Come on young buck. We're going to the roof for a min. "You can hang with us today."

TNT, Spider and Q-Dog started up the last flight of stairs when TNT turned to Q-Dog and said that if he came all the way to the roof he was moving up to the Big Boy league. They stated that if he wasn't ready for this he could go back downstairs. Q-Dog stated that he was ready.

Q-Dog seemed to get a sense of fatherly love coming from both Spider and TNT.They always gave him money when he didn't have enough to go to the movies or the game with the rest of the boys. They used to come to his school basketball games and cheer him on. Little did he know that both Spider and TNT knew his real father. They were in his fathers' crew. Q-Dogs father was a true Fort Villa Gangster that loved his family. When Q-Dog was 2 years old his father walked in and found his mother in bed with an old boyfriend. He killed the boyfriend with 2 shots to the head but let his mother live because of how deep his love was for her and his family. As his father was being sentenced in court for the murder, he overtook one of the court bailiff's gun at the trail and shot himself in the head, killing himself instantly. When they searched his belongings back in his cell there was a departing letter saying that he wouldn't be able to live in jail thinking about what had already happened and what his mind would make happen while he was locked up. He stated his love for his wife and family and asked them for his forgiveness. He asked that his two best friends help look over his family until his wife found another provider. Those two friends were TNT and Spider. Fort Villa Legions.

No it's ok .I want to chill with both of you guys Q- Dog replied. Hey what's that all wrapped up that you didn't want me to throw away", Q-Dog asked. It's what we call a bird. Cocaine. A Lot of it answered Spider. Do you know who it belongs to? Q-Dog knew right away that the package was probably what Jose was looking for. He didn't say a word. In fact Q-Dog said "naw, I don't know". "Don't worry, you and your people are gonna be ok. Come on we're here, TNT said as they reached the door to the roof.

As the roof door opened and they started walking in, there was an eerie feeling of death in the air. The only description of that would be the smell of old garbage cans full of a month's worth of garbage. Bad. Real bad!!!

"Look at da blood clod. I man crapped right in um pants. Smelling up the ross clad city, 'Bumma clod.", said Rude Boy, the Jamaican man that lived downstairs from Q-Dog.Yea that dirt bag knows his time is coming to an end. We don't mess around in the Fort, negro, Said Dead Eye. He lived on the first floor. Both were one of Top Cats soldiers.

Let's get this episode over with Playa's. I got girls to

look after, Raheem said in a smooth pimp voice.

Ok, let's get it on. This dirt bag is guilty of committing a major hood offense on Fort Green soil. That was Top Cat talking. The boss of the hood, supplier and protector. As well as Q-Dogs older cousin on his fathers' side. At that point Q-Dog was witnessing a court that was held in the hood. The accused, his victim, judge and jury. "What we have is a failure to respect the codes of our hood"! Top Cat bellowed.

"Let's do what it do, bruh", came from Dead Eye, one of Top Cats hitmen.With that, Top Cat motioned to a new recruit in his crew and handed him a gun. Top Cat continued to speak on the infractions this man committed. This dirtbag took it upon himself to come into our hood and not only disrespect the hood but the women in our hood as well. This man has been beating on this sister here, my cousin, on a constant basis. Look at her. As everyone turned and focused on the sister, she was in very bad shape. Her eyes were nearly shut from brutal punches to the face. Her lips were swollen so bad that she couldn't even talk. Her left ear was swollen 5 times its original size. The results from a few swift kicks to the head with over-sized Timberland boots. She was brutally beaten. When Q-Dog looked at her his thought was there is no reason for a man to beat on any women. Top Cat told everyone that this man damaged this woman and needed to pay. He then told the gunman to kill him. There was hesitation in the new recruit to follow the order. Everyone seeing that this was hard for the rookie gunman started encouraging him to kill him. "Shoot that dirt bag!". "He doesn't deserve to live!". With all the encouragement the gunman couldn't do it.Q-Dog was standing next to the gunman. His adrenaline was racing as he too waited to see what was going to happen next. That's when Top Cat started screaming, "Shoot him! Shoot, "shoot him! This man is beating on our woman. Not only does he beat on women, but he beats on their children too! When Q-Dog heard that he blacked out.Without realizing what he was doing Q-Dog snatched the gun from the man ,aimed and unloaded eight rounds into the midsection of the man on his knees. Everyone started tripping out. Yelling and screaming. Top Cat and Spider grabbed Q-Dog, got the gun and hurried him downstairs to Spiders apt. "WOW Q-Dog you ok? You wigged out man, said Spider. "Yea kid what's really up", asked Top Cat. You were a One Man Army up there.Q-Dog stayed quiet. As if he was scared to say anything. Spider then said, "You shot that dirt bag like that was your mother he beat up. Still Q-Dog didn't say anything. "Is that what it is Q-Dog? That dirt bag is beating your mother? Still Q-Dog did or said nothing. "Is he beating on you and your sister too? Top Cat asked. That's when Q-Dog broke down and started crying.

"Don't worry Q-Dog, it's gonna be ok. Top Cat said as he looked at Spider with eyes that said, "Handle that bruh!".

Later that evening Q-Dog, his mother and his sister were sitting around the T.V. in the living room, when they heard the key in the door . Everyone tensed up. The first thing that went through Q-Dogs mom's mind was, "Oh my God, here he comes. This man is going to kill us all. Q-Dog was thinking that if he starts some stuff tonight he was going to run downstairs and get Spider and TNT to kill him.

Jose finally entered and the climate was chilling and very disturbing. To everyone's surprise Jose spoke with a calm voice as if nothing ever happened. In fact he seemed very remorseful. José bent down and gave his wife a kiss on the forehead. She was shocked. What has come over him? Whatever the case he was a perfect gentle man. The perfect stand in father. All American provider.

Q-Dog later found out that Spider and the guys went to the pool hall that Jose hangs out at to sell drugs and stuck a 9mm gun in his mouth. They introduced themselves as Q-Dogs uncles and told him if Q-Dog or any of the family members get as much as a hangnail on them, then he took the gun out his mouth, pointed the gun at the bar and shot about 4 bottles up. "Comprende Jose?"

Q-dog and his family never had a problem from Jose again. The events of that day gave Q-Dog the confidence that with the right emotions and attitude he could make people react the way he wanted and he didn't have any fear anymore. The start of a character defect that got him in a hospital bed clinging to his life. He had the spirit of a One Man Army.

Chapter 3

TRIALS AND TRIBULATIONS

As Blue was sitting on the fire escape outside of the window of his apartment, the night breeze was so refreshing to his skin. His girl, Sharell, was lying on her back with her head in his lap, looking at the stars. Blue had a sense of peace as the night sounds filtered the air. The neon lights of Club Encore were illuminating on Shirelles' skin as Blue thought, "Thank God for Life and another Day to Get It Right". You see, usually Blue and his crew would be outside amongst the hustlers, on artists ,pimps,prostitutes,cops and club hoppers making it do what it do. Getting paid by any means necessary.

Blue had a crew that was loyal to the hood, but most importantly they had a loyalty that was to each other. The fact of the matter is that Blue had a crew that was a thinking crew. They were very smart. Each move that they made was well thought out. If someone had an idea they would feed it to the crew, then bring it to Blue. He would put the finishing touches on it and if it made cents they would get dollars.

Blue and Sharell had been together for about one year now in a one bedroom apartment. They were a young couple in love and Sharrell always had the dream of one day marrying Blue.Becoming his wife. Blue was at one of the first major crossroads of his life. His love for Sharell and his loyalty to his crew. He loved them both and Sharell knew this. She was ok with that because she loved him deeply. She stood by his side and everything he was about. But that wasn't enough for Blue. He gave his word to both Sharell and his crew. He knew he couldn't live the life he was living and make a family with Sharell at the same time. What was he going to do? "A penny for your thoughts", Sharrell said to Blue as she looked up into Blues' eyes. "Wow , is that all I'm worth is a penny"? "Baby you're worth all the money I have plus all the money I owe everybody else. They both laughed as Blue picked up her head and gave her a deep passionate kiss.

"I've been thinking about changing the way we make money baby" Blue told Sharell as he stared into her eyes. "What's on your mind Papi"? Well whatever we do, I want to do it the legal way". No guns, no robbing, no stealing or conning. I don't know how the crew is going to take it, or even you for that matter. If we do it the way I envision it ,we wouldn't be pulling in as much money so we wouldn't be living as large. One thing for sure is I got to follow my spirit and my spirit is telling me to get right. Blue, baby as long as I'm with you and you continue to share your love and spirit with me it doesn't matter how large we live. I'm down with you for whatever,Sharell told him.

I'm happy to hear that because I'm calling a meeting tonight with the crew baby. "We'll see how it goes", Blue said as they both got up and climbed off the fire escape into the window of their apartment.

Blue and Sharell took a cab to 34th st and Power rd. That area was named Restaurant Row. Eat shops on both sides of the street. The meeting tonight was to be at BeefSteak Charlie's. A well known restaurant in the downtown area. Every one of the crews' decision makers were present at this meeting. Blue, Q- Dog, Tookie , Sharell , Lollipop ,LD and Paulie. Learning more about himself spiritually Blue started the meeting with a prayer. Little did he know that as he was transforming, and so was his crew. All from his lead and example. After the prayer Blue started the meeting with actual facts from the population of the immediate area, to the spending power of all the commuters male and female. Blue showed everyone the example of Mr. FootLong. Mr. Footlong started his business about 5 years ago on the corner of Wells Ave. It was a good location right by the expressway. A lot of traffic.

Mr. FootLong started selling Coney Island Hot Dogs in front of his two room ranch style home. His stand was no bigger than 4' by 6' with two compartments . One for hotdogs and the other for onions and buns. He had a regular ice cooler on the side for cold drinks. Now with organization and a hard working family (sons, daughters, and his wife), five years later they converted their two bedroom home into a restaurant seating 100 people. He purchased the two acres next to him and built a five room,2 ½ bath, 2 car garage, living room, dining room ,full finished basement and a 16' x 32'in the ground swimming pool.

Everyone listening to Blue knew what he was talking about , because they couldn't pass Mr. Foot Long without stopping and ordering 2 foot longs with heavy onions, mustard ,ketchup, and a drink. They also realized they helped pay for the luxuries that his family achieved. "So what are we going to do , "sell hotdogs", asked Paulie, the crew's funnyman. "Naw Paulie , but I got a plan that will push us faster and higher than his elevation".

Blue started explaining his plan. Taking the money that the crew had and investing it in some merchandise for our neighborhood peeps. He said that if they bought some men, women and children clothes and shoes , and rented the corner store from Miss Sally , they would be there. The only stores in the hood were liquor stores, candy stores, number spots, drug spots and strip joints. If you wanted to buy any clothes you had to go downtown or uptown which was one bus and two trains away. Not to mention you were going to pay crazy prices for them. Blue explained how they would keep the cost of the merchandise down and service the four project complexes right away. Especially if their product was tight. Everybody in the crew was down. They knew it was a good idea. They were ready and excited.

Blue noticed Q-Dog was uneasy the entire meeting. "What's up Q-Dog?", Blue asked as he looked into Q-Dogs face . Q-Dog looked at Blue as if he was ready to explode. "Yo Blue I need to talk to you, one on one after the meeting.

“No problem , I got you man”. When the meeting was over everybody went their ways excited and ready for the new change.

“What’s up, Q-Dog? “Look like you got a lot on your mind”. “Yea man , it’s my mom. She’s losing her house. She wasn’t able to keep up the 2nd mortgage after she lost her job. Mom kept this from me. I found out one day when I was home and a bank rep came over. They said she had 5 days to pay or get out. How much does she owe, asked Blue”? $22,000.00 Q-Dog replied, and they want every penny.

“WOW” ,said Blue. We don’t have that , but we got to do something for mom. Blue took that news hard as if it were his own mother. That’s how everyone in the crew was with each other. Family. “Well I got a plan but after that meeting we just had you’re not going to want to hear it Q-Dog said. “Forget that”, said Blue “what is it”?

“I know where we could get that much money plus some”. Where , asked Blue”? Right where we had our meeting at tonight ,Q- Dog told him. “BeefSteak Charlie's” Blue said as he focused on the big knot that came in the pit of his stomach. Q-Dog needed the help and Blue was down to assist. All kind of things were going on in Blues head. After all the planning of doing things the right way ,they didn’t have the money and there was only one way to get it. What did you have in mind Blue asked Q-Dog. Thats when Q-Dog started revealing his plan. Every Saturday night at BeefSteak Charlies they always have Thursday, Friday, and Saturday night money drops on deck at one time. They put it all in the freezer for the manager on Sunday morning to make the bank drop of the weekend. The good thing is they leave the alarms off when they leave that night for the carpet cleaners to come in and work .My baby momma put me up on game. She used to work there.

That's all Blue had to hear. He had the plan already worked out in his head. Ok Q-Dog, go home and tell mom we got her. It's going to be alright. "Blue went home and told Sharell. Sharell didn't like the idea but she knew Blue was going on with it. She knew he loved Q-Dog like a brother and that he was going to make something happen. She also knew that there was no question that she was going to be a part of it.

Blue explained the plan. The last workers to leave the spot was 11:00pm and the carpet cleaners were scheduled to come in at 1:00am.They were going to steal a carpet cleaning van,uniforms,pull up and break into the back door. They could be in and out in 15 minutes. So it was on. Saturday was it.

10:00 Saturday night , everything was in place. Although the rest of the crew was down to do the job, it would be easier with only three, in uniform and a carpet cleaning van.11:00 they were in place. As they watched the last workers leave and the coast was clear they moved in to go to work.

Working like a well oiled machine ,they went into action. Keep in mind they also had fake IDs in case of getting popped by the cops. Blue always had a good plan. In case they got popped, without evidence or witnesses, with a clean fake ID's it's easier to get out of lock up in 72 hours. Q-Dog took a 5 lb sledge hammer and broke the lock on the back door so clean that it didn't even look like a forced entry. They went in knowing the layout of the restaurant. They went right to the freezer. They looked around for about seven minutes when they found the money. It was in three money bags. They were working with the lights of the kitchen on. Why not? They were supposed to be there. They were cleaning the carpet. As they were coming out of the freezer Blue looked toward the front and he saw about three flashlight beams shining in the front windows. Right away Blue thought , Unbelievable! Change your old ways started running through his mind. People ,places and things. Everything was hitting him in his head, right away. How can you say you want to change your life around and don't hold on to your Faith that the creator put in you. Going back and doing the same thing you always did. That's a sign of insanity. He needed to do some quick thinking and that meant now.

"That's the cops" Blue said. "What should we do?", asked Sharell. Without thinking twice Blue took off his overalls, stashed them into the garbage bin. He told Sharell to stash as much money in her girdle as she could. (He always told Sharrell to wear girdles on jobs and now she knew why.)Sharell started stashing. Being a little lady you couldn't tell she stashed stacks in her underpants, that's when they heard the phrase they all will never forget. "This is the Police". "Come out with your hands raised high above your heads". That's when Q-Dog and Sharell got the shock of their lives. Blue motioned for them to lie down on the ground , face down. As Sharell got down on the ground she looked up at Blue with tears in her eyes. As he looked back down at her Sharell said “Papi, please, don’t do it like this”.

“Baby, Yo, it’s ok. We rehearsed this ever since you and I been getting down like this,” Blue told Sharell. “You know what to do”.Q-Dog on the other hand was confused. “What’s up Blue”? Just lay down on the ground Q-Dog , follow Shirelles' lead, we don’t have much time, Blue instructed. “Forget that man”,Q-Dog responded. With quick reflexes Blue pulled a gun out from under his shirt and hit Q-Dog in the eye yelling , “Get on the floor man and I’m not playing”. Q-Dog went down hard holding his eye as Sharell said “stay down Q-Dog, it’s the only way. This is the way that Blue wants it. “Just follow my lead”. Blue then yelled “I’m coming out!” Blue looked at Sharell and Q-Dog and said, “it’s ok. It’s the best way”. Blue didn’t want his girl doing any jail time. So he was going to take it all. Blue always had a backup plan and this was it. I’m coming out. Blue yelled again. Don’t shoot I’m coming out.

Blue came out of the back, hands raised high in the air after he threw the gun down. The police jumped on Blue, beating him as he knelt on the ground. The rest ran in for Sharell and Q-Dog. When they got to them , Sharell started screaming like she had lost it all. Seeing both of them in carpet cleaning uniforms and Q-Dog with a busted eye ,the police quickly put it all together. Blue had surprised the cleaning crew. The police searched Q-Dog but Sharell was putting on such an Academy Award Winning act they totally forgot to search her. They took both their statements , false ID’s and told them they would get back with them if they needed them. Since the alarm was never set it didn't go off so the real owner wasn't alerted. That's when Sharell saw how smart Blue was. He had Paulie and LD standing by watching everything. They came running up like they were the owners. They took statements from everyone and let them all go.

In the meantime , Blue was arrested for armed robbery, burglary and assault. Blue copped out to a 1 to 3 year sentence. In following instructions, Sharell had stuffed about $75,000.,00 in her girdle. Blue instructed Sharell to pay off Q-Dogs' mom's bills with extras. Sharell moved back to her moms house and started preparing herself and the crew for Blues return. Blue being jailed hurt everyone, but they were loyal to Blue. They followed instructions. Blue always told them that God was always in control of them.

That's when Sharell started getting real respect from the crew. She conditioned them as if Blue was right there running operations himself. They worked hard getting clean and staying clean. Sharrell had her two close girls working by her side, Lollipop and LD. Two hard working fly girls that didn't take no mess and always got the job done, whatever it was. Loyal to Sharell and the game. Respected by all. Sharell took the remaining money invested in Tee Shirts and women's pocketbooks. Before you knew it they moved up to incense, oils, CD's and baby clothes. Q-Dog took Blues' time hard. His partner was doing time for helping his mother. Q-Dog took care of whatever Sharell or her family needed. Blue was his partner for life. He owed him.

Due to the violence of the crime, Blue had to max out and do the entire 3 years. Everyone including Sharell went through major trials and tribulations during the course of Blue's incarcerations. In fact Sharell went through a personal trial that she kept from Blue while he was in jail. She kept it from him because she didn't want him to trip while he was locked up. She knew she would have to reveal to him soon after he returned home because it was heavy on her spirit. One thing for sure was that they stayed strong on staying clean and preparing for Blue to get out. Together all of them would start a righteous way of life.

Blue finally got out. He , Sharell and the crew continued their new life of a drug free productive way of living. Trials and tribulations continue to come, but when they come and you are striving to do the right thing it may be a little pain, but it's a good pain. Never forget that the Creator is always present.

Chapter 4

No Matter What

It's the winter and super bowl time. It was so cold that the only thing moving outside was the wind. There were 12 foot snow drifts on the side of all the houses on the block. In fact , the plows hadn't come through yet. Everybody in the neighborhood was completely snowed in.There was one thing for sure. It was Super Bowl time.

We were all at my partner's house, big C's. There were about 10 of us there. I couldn't tell you how all of us got here in this storm, but we were here.Big C was always having something at his House. We always had what we thought was fun while we were in our drug addiction but now that we were all clean we saw how crazy we really were.
By the way it must be said that we all used drugs together. Now that we were clean we were all part of the live and let die group. Our motto was "We live to let the drugs die". Before we got clean off drugs we used to have it all.

Whatever drugs you wanted we had it.Now here we are sitting around yelling and screaming at the T.V. while eating fish and chips, washing it down with sweet iced tea. Enjoying life without drugging. Thanking God for life.

"Man I got a burning desire I have to get off my chest" Blue yelled at the crew. Not now Gee. Wait till the game is over Q-Dog replied. Q-Dog had that serious "Don't mess with me" look on his face as did everyone else . Blue thought "I don't believe this. I got some heavy stuff on my mind and all my boys are thinking about is this crazy game? The crew couldn't hold it in any longer and broke into a deep hard laugh inviting Blue to spill his guts. Blue laughed it off and did just that. Started spitting it out.
Ever since I lost my job and had to move into my in-laws basement I've been the go to man, son, brother and boyfriend, but lately I've had to be a daily referee. You see Ahmad and Rainbow are my girlfriend's brothers. Two brothers that share a love-hate relationship.

Ahmad is a 16 year old lost boy. The middle child of a sibling group of 6.Because of not having a father at home and an older brother with another agenda that did not include him,Ahmad found love in the streets. Ahmad started getting high on weed at age 11. That's the area that most of the fights came from. Rainbow is a 23 year old gang banger that suffers from the disease of epileptic. When their father left them when Rainbow was 10 years old he too went to the streets and found love. His love came from the gangs.Rainbow also took on the role of head of household. Man of the house.

Seems to me you need to get on the serenity prayer and accept the things that you cannot change, Q-Dog said with a serious concerned look. Yea but I believe I can change something and that's the way Ahmad sees me now. Ahmad looked up to me before I got clean and he always wanted to be like me. Back then I was a pistol totten, drug abuser that ran into any spot, store or home, held the occupants at bay and took whatever I wanted in order to survive. Well you shouldn't have a problem with that because you sure are working a good clean 12 step program, said Tookie. That's all good but he already has a taste of the streets in him and he loves it, and with everything that comes with it.If I can get him to return the focus on me a change may be possible .I would show him what my higher power has done for me and if he submitted his life ,his would get better too. Just keep doing what you're doing. He'll see it.Don't forget you both live in the same house, Q-Dog said with an encouraging statement. You know that's all good but I'm hearing more. What's really going on Blue? Tookie asked. Yea it is something else. Rainbow gets physical when Ahmad comes home high. I'm afraid one of them is really going to get hurt.Yea man.Those two make a deadly cominanation.A gang banger on meds and a young Yoda, he just doesn't give a darn, said Q-Dog. You right Q-Dog, one day they're gonna lock up like two pit bulls.

At that point the room burst into a chorus of jubilation as well as discussion. There was an interception on the defending two-yard line that resulted in a 90-yard return.

Ten blocks from where the guys were watching the game all chaos was starting to unfold.

I told you man, don't come in maws house all messed up,

high as a kite. Get Yo butt up and get the heck out!!!! yelled Rainbow at Ahmad.I ain't going no place this ain't your house and I ain't high. Bull , Rainbow screamed. Just at that moment Blues girl stepped in the middle of them both. Pushing both of her brothers apart trying to keep peace in the house.

Blues girl is named Sharell.Sharell is petite , with a chestnut color complexion. Although Sharell was little she still had a very shapely figure. About 5 foot 2 inches tall and 125 pounds. Her stance was proud like a peacock and although slightly bow legged, she had the grace and elegance of a Lippenhimer show horse at the peak of their performance. A proud thoroughbred.
Now every coin has two sides to it. Growing up in the hood, being the oldest girl in the house without a father figure, she had the fight of a mother grizzly bear protecting her cubs. Very fierce and powerful. After all that being said, Sharell had a little secret she and Blue was keeping. They were the only two that knew she was 7 months pregnant with their first child on the way. With her small figure and it being winter she was able to conceal the pregnancy from everyone under warm winter clothing.

Yawl cut this out! I'm tired of both of you with this crap . Mommy just needs to come in here and put both of you out of her house Sharell yelled. We ain't got to wait for maw I'm going to put this trash out of the house by myself, Rainbow screamed back.
Forget you Rainbow . I took my last butt kicking from you. That action stops right here.Right now Ahmad snapped back. The noise level had gotten so loud that it woke Ms. Dixon out

of her sleep. MS. Dixon is Mamma. She‘s a hard working black woman that is the glue that has kept her family together. As they all got older it seemed as though it was slowly falling apart from the infiltration of vices and personalities of the outside world. It has gotten very uncomfortable lately. Rainbow was beating up on Ahmad for smoking weed , when in fact he was smoking himself. Ahmad was smoking weed , making bad decisions on top of failing in school. Ms. Dixon has it hard but Blue and Sharell have made it easier by living there. The only bad thing was that they couldn't be there all the time. They had a life of their own.

All right all of you, yelled Ms. Dixon. If I hear another word from any of you I'll call the cops and have them put all of you out of my house. I mean it too.

When Ms Dixon spoke it seemed to be effective. Everyone split up and went their separate ways. Ahmad went into his room, which was next to the den on the first level. Rainbow went to his room which was located on the basement level next to the room Blue and Sharell shared. Sharell went upstairs in the living room to use the phone to call Blue. The snow storm was getting worse and she had an eerie feeling about the night.

Hello? Big C said as he answered the phone. Yes hello may I speak to Blue? Recognizing the voice Big C said, "what's up Sharell? This is C. Hey C. You know that Blue and I had to move back to my mother's house. I hope we won't be here long. With a strong testimony Big C said, prayer and hard work will get you there. Don't forget you and I both know that Blue ain't nobody's slow leak. You couldn't keep him down when he was leading us in the wrong direction. Now that he's understanding his higher power and working to build, other than destroy, his blessing will come pouring down. As long as you continue to be his strong help meet , you're gonna receive those blessings as well.

Oh yea don't forget I ain't going to be too far from yawl. I need all the blessings I can get too. If I'm close and loyal I might receive some too. Both Big and Sharell started laughing because they both realized the change in their lives when they started doing all the right things for the right reasons. Then Sharell thanked God for putting blue in her life.

You see , if there were a couple on earth that deserved the couple of the century award it would go to Sharell and Blue. Blue loved Sharell to the end of the world. They knew each other since the age of 10 years old. Blue was always a go getta. When Sharells family moved to the block, Blue claimed Sharell and they been a couple ever since. Sharell on the same token was the female side of Blue. His female mirror image. What the crew admired most about Sharell was not her beauty, smarts, sexy walk or ability to make that money. Although all that counts . Her strongest assets was her loyalty to her man. She was down for her man. Whatever it was. Her loyalty to Blue was as strong as a bond between a mother and her newborn child.Unsepterable.When they was in the street life and drug addiction the crew had to sometimes pull little Sha (that's what the crew called her) off other crews that was pushing up on Blue too close. They had to get her out of the way in order to handle whatever problem it was. Now that the crew was out of the streets pursuing the right things, drugs free, she just re-routed her energies in another direction. She stays on top of not only Blue but also the whole crew. She helped keep the love going. She makes sure the crew doesn't miss any 12 step meetings. They hadn't missed any 12 step conventions since they were clean. If she sees someone slipping she'll get right in that ass before they fall. The crew loved both of them to death and were loyal to them both and the fellowship.

Yo Blue it's for you, Big C screamed over all the loud talking. Hello this is Blue. Hey baby is me.Rainbow and Ahmad is at it again. I wish you were here. I got a bad feeling tonight. Blue heard a lot of noise in the background and asked Sharell what was going on. Who's making all that noise, he asked. Ahmad, she said as if he didn't know. Put him on the phone baby, let me talk to him. Sharell called Ahmad over and handed him the phone. Peace God, Ahmad said. Peace Ahmad what's going on over there. This nigger…. Blue quickly stopped Ahmad and said nigger?Yo Ahmad we vowed that we wouldn't use those types of names describing our brothers and sisters no matter how messed up they are. My bad Ahmad answered. Well Rainbow came in thinking he was gonna come in here and handle me like he always does. That action is over, Ahmad said . Ahmad you been smoking asked Blue.Yeah man.Me and my girl smoked a blunt earlier. He ain't bout to diss me no more man.In front of my girl too. Heck no. Blue quickly took over the conversation. Ahmad look , for right now can you and your girl just go in your room and chill until I come. When I get there we're all gonna sit down and get this mess right. Yeah ok Ahmad said. But if …but if nothing man, Blue snapped. Ok Blue. Peace man. See you when you get here. All right Blue said. Let me speak back to Sharell. As Ahmad was handing the phone back to Sharell, Blue heard him say," that nut better keep his hands to himself tonight". I got something for his butt if he doesn't. See what I'm saying

Sharell said. It just doesn't feel right tonight baby.Ahmad looks like he's doing more than just smoking blunts. I'll handle everything when I get back Blue told Sharell with a comforting tone. What's he doing now Blue asked. With a worried voice Sharell answered he's going into his room with his girlfriend. Good .Ok baby just listen out and if anything starts up again give me a call. At that point they both exchanged their love for each other and hung the phone up.

No sooner than the hanging up of the phone the drama started to unleash itself once again. Ahmad went into the living room and started playing the radio with the volume up so loud it could have broken all the windows in the house. He was singing to the top of his lungs as if trying to incite Rainbow into a confrontation. Now take heed that Rainbow was no little punk. He's 6'3" tall and very muscular. He bench presses 450 lbs. and has been shot 4 times in gang wars. In fact he's the head of one of the most feared gangs in the city.

Rainbow on the other hand, trying to obey his mothers wishes to keep peace, came upstairs, walked into the living room and turned down the music saying, ok enough is enough. Rainbow go back into your little hole and leave us alone, Ahmad said in an intimidating voice. While walking back to his room Rainbow in the spirit that not only the house knows but also the entire neighborhood have witnessed simply said yeah ok Ahmad , ok . This spirit we're talking about is the quiet before the storm one. Whenever Rainbow is in this spirit , he is most vulnerable. This is the time to attack him. If you don't and the transformation continues you'd better get out of the way. He comes out like a school of

Piranha fish. Fast and deadly. Destroying everything in its path. Rainbow finally got to his room , shut the door , laid on his bed and looked at his clock. It was 8.30 pm.

Earlier when Sharell was talking to Blue she stated that it looked like Ahmad was smoking more than blunts. Well she was right. About 12:00 noon Ahmad and his girlfriend had popped 2 Extacy pills each. He was rolling off of X and it was taking over him at this time. Waiting until he knew Rainbow was comfortable:

Man forget Rainbow. I pay bills around here too. That's when Ahmad turned the music up so high it could have awakened the dead. At that very instant Rainbow and Ahmad broke out running like two race horses bolting out of the starting gates in the Kentucky Derby. Ahmad ran to the kitchen fumbling around the silver drawer searching for a knife. Rainbow came charging out of his room like a raging bull snorting from the nostrils with bloodshot eyes. Sharell was in the living room when it all started and her reflexes made her move in Ahmad's direction screaming Ahmad no. Oh God no Ahmad. As big as Rainbow was he scaled the steps like a squirrel going up a tree, not missing a beat. By the time Rainbow had gotten closer to the top step Ahmad met him. Ahmad's right hand raised high above his head brandishing the very knife that just recently carved the thanksgiving turkey. A nine inch long, two inch wide turkey knife ,now turned into an assault weapon.

Ahmad came down hard. Hitting Rainbow on his left side right between his shoulder and his neck. Sharell let out a loud scream ,"God no". "God no". The knife hit Rainbow in his jugular vein. It went in deep and punctured his lung. Blood was squirting out like a water balloon with a pin hole in it.The blood was going everywhere. On the walls, ceiling, everywhere. With Rainbow's big frame and size, his momentum carried him past Ahmad right into the middle of the kitchen.

As Rainbow stood in the kitchen holding his neck with his back to Sharell and Ahmad, he slowly turned back around holding a nickel plated, pearl handle 9mm pistol. He aimed and shot as he fell to the kitchen floor, blood flowing from his body.

Ms. Dixon was in the basement washing clothes when she heard the first screams. By the time she got to the kitchen there they were. Her three children. Rainbow in a pool of blood in the middle of the kitchen floor on his back and Ahmad sitting on the kitchen floor holding his sisters head in his lap crying and screaming mommy I'm sorry, I'm sorry.Sharell was shot. Bullet wound on her left side. At that point Ms. Dixon's body went into overload and she fainted. Falling out right on top of her daughter.

Ms. Dixons youngest daughter April ,13 years old, ran downstairs and saw her entire family on the kitchen floor with blood everywhere. She quickly grabbed the phone to call the one person next to her mother that she felt protected by and that was Blue.

Now as everyone was enjoying the game, Blue felt his phone vibrating. He looked at the caller id and it said Boo. That would be Sharell. At first he wasn't going to answer it right away but a feeling came over him so he answered it.Hey Boo what's up? April started screaming into the phone.Not being able to understand what was said, much less who was talking , Blue just hung up the phone and looked at the crew and said" something is wrong at the house", somebody give me a ride. Seeing the seriousness of Blues face Big C said 'yo I'll give you one. The crew always was one for all and all for one. They all piled into C's Yukon Xl and got down to the house in a matter of minutes. When they pulled up to the yard it was filled with people from the hood. Nosey rubber neckers.The front door was wide open. Not knowing what happened, Blue ran right past Ms. Dixon and Ahmad hugging each other crying. At the very time Blue got there the emergency team pulled up. Cops right behind them. Blue got in first, noticing there were people in the house he didn't even know. He went upstairs to the kitchen and that's when his heart almost fell out of his mouth. He saw Rainbow in a pool of blood and the love of his life Sharell , lying halfway in the kitchen and living room floor. Blue went insane. Who did this!.They got to die, Blue thought. That's when the medics and cops rushed in.The cops grabbed Blue, dragged him out the front door and handcuffed him. With all the threats coming from Blue they didn't know if he was the attacker or not so they subdued him until they put all the pieces together.

The medics worked on both Rainbow and Sharell.Blue was observing everything from the back of the police car now. He was held in the car because he had become very unmanageable. Blue watched a scene that he and his crew saw over and over in the hood. Only this time it hit home .Right on his block. In his very own family. In fact, right in his very own bed. Blue started replaying in his head how he should have been there instead of watching the game. If he had been a better role model then maybe things would have been different.

Blue saw a common move when someone dies at the scene. The tape is pulled out to secure the area. The corina van comes and within minutes the area is clean of its vitims.Blue started praying profusely.Tears rolling out of his eyes like a broken water faucet, non stop.Blue continued to ask god to save his wife and unborn child . With the light from the corner pole being the only one on in the block, visibility was very hard, but Blue kept the keen eagle eye on the front door and everything that was moving.

Time doesn't wait for nobody but it sure can take its sweet time .The anticipation of not knowing was making Blue sicker and sicker . Finally the emergency crew came out rolling two gurneys. They were so fast nobody could see anything. They put the two bodies in the ambulance, turned on the lights and headed for Mercy hospital. About five minutes later the coroner came out with a body bag zipped up completely. It was thrown in the back of the van and hauled off. As Blues mind was trying to process all that he witnessed he began to fade out until he was completely gone. Total blackout.

When Blue regained consciousness he woke up looking at Q-Dog, Tookie, Big C, and Sharells sister April. Blue was in the Mercy Emergency ward. He had passed out. They had him in the hallway, on a gurney.The first thing he asked was how was Sharell doing? Where was she? April looking down at Blue with tears in her eyes said that Sharell asked her to come down and get him. She was in the intensive care unit. She said to hurry. April told Blue that Sharell wanted to see everybody, but she wanted to see him first.

Having heard enough, Blue got off the gurney, motioned to the crew and told April to lead the way. As they got closer to the front desk of the ICU ward, Blue and everyone could see a couple arguing back and forth with the nurses. "Why can't I see him?". He's my best friend. I was in the car when we ran off the road. The response from the nurse was "I'm sorry but we can only let in immediate family members . Blue grabbed April's hand and headed to the desk. April pulled Blues hand hard causing him to stop in his tracks. Blue turned back to

April and she said “Blue Sharell said to tell you “no matter what”.

We came to see Sharell Dixon, Blue told the nurse .Ok we can only let in immediate family. Yes I know, I’m her husband. April looked surprised at Blue as he handed her a piece of paper out of his wallet. It was a marriage certificate between her sister and Blue. April really loved Blue. She looked up to Blue like the older brother she wished she had. Rainbow and Ahmad didn’t have the time for her .She gave Blue a loving smile and they started in.The rest of the crew sat down in the available chairs in the waiting area.

When April and Blue entered Sharells room Blue noticed that she was hooked up to all kind of stuff. The only sounds in the room was the sounds coming from the heart monitor and the swooshing sounds of the oxygen machine. The wells in Blues eyes started filling up ready to overflow. He never saw his love so helpless. It was too much for him to bear and the tears started pouring out as he sat down by his Queen. “Please God don’t take my Boo from me," he thought. We’ve been together since we were 10 years old. She been my girl for 17 years. I don’t know what I’d do without her. As Blue was remembering the past with his head embedded in his hands, shielding his emotions from April he heard a voice so familiar say “hey Popi”. A feeling of joy came over him. He looked up and saw his queen looking up at him smiling. Sharell said “Te Amo Popi”. Trying to fight the tears back blue said “I love you too Mommy.

Baby I need you to listen to me closely ok, Sharell said. Blue told Sharell to save her strength for later. That’s when Sharell responded saying “baby this is Very important and I need you to listen”. Blue gave her his undivided attention. I want you to call the nurse. She’s waiting for us to call her .

Blue did as she wished. Blue leaned over to Sharell and kissed her on the forehead. Seeing his wife so helpless was wrecking him .There was a light knock at the door and they came in.The nurse and a small bundle of joy. A baby wrapped in a pink blanket. The nurse gave the baby to Sharell. With all that was going on Blue totally forgot that they were expecting a baby. He smiled down at both mother and child. Blue had a smile so bright it could have put the sun out. Her name is Princess, Sharell said and she is healthy as could be. Looking at her, Blue saw that his daughter looked just like her mother. So much like her at birth it was scary.

Sharell continued to talk to Blue and April. With her baby in her arms she started telling them how she had gotten shot by the 9mm gun that Rainbow shot. The bullet went in her upper left chest, tearing arteries, lungs and had major internal damage. She explained that the doctor said the internal bleeding and damage was so severe that she was not going to make it through the night. Blue didn't want to hear that. This is a hospital. Somebody here could make her better.Somebody could fix her back to health. Make her whole again. God please do something he thought. I've changed my wicked ways. Don't do this to me Blue thought. Please God. Please.

Forget that Blue shouted. I'm going to get the doctor. "No," Sharell shouted. We may not have that much time. I've got to talk to you now. Blue saw how serious Sharell looked and gave her all of his attention. Popi when we first met at age ten I knew I wanted to be your girl. Blue started to respond but Sharell quieted his intentions. I fell in love with you at an early age. Never wanting to be apart from you. We've done some crazy things together from using drugs, robbery, burglary, so many things. I must say that I don't regret anything we've done together. Right now I'm so proud of you. You made a complete turnaround. You were the first one of the crew to stop using drugs. Persuading the rest of us to follow your lead and stop too. All of us.

You were our leader when we were in the underworld right to continue leading us in the right way of living a drug free productive life. I could not ask for a better husband. I'm proud to be your wife. Most importantly I could not have picked a better father for my child.

As Blue and April listened, Sharells strength was getting weaker and weaker but she held off Blue's request to slow down and continued on.

Poppi I know the creator is calling me.I can hear him louder and louder as the seconds tick on. I want you to promise me you will take care of Princess and my sister April with the love and respect you always gave me. No matter what. If you can promise me that, not only will my spirit be pleased but I know our Creator will be pleased as well. With tears flowing out of everyone's eyes, Sharell, April, Blue and even the baby Princess, Blue told Sharell "I promise no matter what.

Sharell asked Blue to go out and get the rest of the crew. Blue went out to the waiting area and motioned for the crew to come quickly. The nurse didn't even try to stop them .one by one they filed in. Each giving mother and child a kiss on their forehead.When everyone got in Sharell asked them all to form a circle around her bed. Sharell told them how proud she was of them in their recovery off drugs and staying strong doing the right things for the right reasons. She wanted everyone to recite the Serenity Prayer with her as they all held hands. Before they started Sharell asked everyone to promise that whatever the outcome of her condition was that they would not use drugs. No matter what!!! They all promised. A promise that pleased her spirit. With tears rolling down everyone's face they held hands in a circle around her bed and started reciting the prayer.

God grant me protection against the things that I cannot change. The courage against the things that I can and the wisdom to know the difference .Amen.

After the prayer everyone was giving each other hugs when they focused on Sharell. She had a heavenly peaceful smile on her face. She was pleased with her loved ones and her spirit was now with her Creactor.The heart monitor flatline. Our loved one had gone home to the Creator.

Chapter 5

Death and Recovery

It's sort of a dry cold in the middle of January. A cold that only those who know can endure. There were many people gathered at First Missionary Baptist Church attending one of the area's biggest funerals. They were all present for Raymond "Rainbow "Dixon and Sharell Dixon Gonzalez's final homecoming .The church was filled to capacity. Standing room only. Many political figures were present as well. Some that were in attendance were the major, chief of police, NAACP, Black Panther Party and many gang members. The most in attendance was the 12 step program family.

If there was anything good about a funeral this one was picture perfect. There were so many flowers around the two caskets the only person that could stand up in that area was the rev. There are about eight rows behind the pulpit for the choir to sit. That section as well as the entire pulpit was filled with flowers. The rev had to stand between the caskets to deliver the eulogy.

Rev. Lyndon knew both Rainbow and Sharell since they were little children in the neighborhood.Rev. Lyndon gave such a prolific sermon on true family love. She tied the sermon into the tragic situation that happened on 12th ave five days ago. She spoke on how Rainbow, Sharell and Ahmad were all working in divine order. Although if we truly believe that our life story has already been written by our creator. We should be able to accept what happens to us in our daily lives. We can determine how our lives go by making the right decisions in God's eyes.Unfortunately this script ended up tragic. We have a family that has lost three of its members. Two members died. One by gunshot the other by knife wound. The third one gone off to serve prison time for the murder of one of the victims. The one that went to jail was only sixteen years old. The victims were his brother and sister.

Each one of the deceased Dixon children made a grave impact in a certain area of God's world. Present in support of rainbow was about one hundred ex inmates, gang members, the mayor, prison officials and believe it or not the chief of police himself. The chief was one of the program speakers. That's when everyone found out that Rainbow had been inspired by his sister Sharell. Not only to change his life around, but to help others to do so too. MS Dixon knew but didn't say anything to any of the family members before Rainbow's death because he made her promise to keep it to herself. Rainbow was a natural born leader. When he saw how Sharell had changed her life following the example of Blue he started sitting with her learning all he could about self empowerment and community development. Rainbow and his gang began going to schools, churches and inner city youth programs teaching on the ills of drugs and gang violence. From what I understand at the time of his death he and many of his peers had stopped getting high. Rainbow's hardest pupil was his brother Ahmad. According to the chief, although Rainbow and Ahmad constantly fought, Rainbow had a deep love for his little brother. Rainbow saw a pattern that Ahmad had taken and he knew he would end up like himself if they didn't stop the insanity now. Rainbow didn't want that for his brother. That's why Rainbow was so hard on Ahmad. Rainbows impact in this tragedy was although he had used drugs, pimped women, robbed, stole, cheated and even murdered was if you summit to change sincerely, with the blessings from your higher power a change of good will come. Rainbow's entire gang vowed to continue to help the major and chief of police in being neighborhood advocates against drugs and crime. In all they vowed to keep Rainbow's dream alive. Although originally from a small town right outside of Atlanta Ga. Sharell impacted the entire world. Sharell had mourners from all parts of the world. Africa, China, Asia, Iran, Alaska, P.R., Brazil, Jamaica, Spain, Turkey, Germany, Australia and every state in America. You see Sharell was a 12 step world committee board member. A group that helped people that are trying to recover from drugs and alcohol addiction. Blue was also of that same group. Sharell joined after blue did. They were like Siamese twins. You couldn't separate them. Blue saw how great Sharell was with helping others. He thought it would be a great opportunity for her to see the world and travel. Sharell did just that during the time Blue was in jail serving time. By the time she had finished her first world tour she had well over 5,000 friends all over God's creation. When she returned she showed how the love she had for her higher power and staying clean could be fun and joyous. The love she shared with blue and the crew was unconditional. Some people have made statements on how both she and Rainbow couldn't reach Ahmad. Sometimes if you stand too close to the light you can't see what else is in the room. That could have been Ahmad's ailment. Some say the middle child syndrome. Nobody knows but the creator and Ahmed.What Ahmad did was totally uncalled for. Keeping it real, the community knew he was under the influence of weed, beer, and ecstasy pills.A deadly combination for a young energetic lost boy. Anybody to that matter would eventually fall while under the influence of all those drugs. The courts allowed Ahmad to come to the funeral. When he first arrived they were outside parked in the car .He was escorted by two heavily armed detectives. The funeral was so large that they weren't going to come in for fear of an unruly emotional situation.

Blue was sitting on the first pew right in front of Sharells' casket holding his newborn daughter. Word kept coming to him that Ahmad was outside sitting in the cop car. Why was everyone bothering him with that? He didn't give a damn about Ahmad. Ahmad was the reason why everyone was here in the first place. Wow Ahmad he thought. Forget them.As Blue was going through those emotional feelings a spirit came over him. He heard a familiar voice but he couldn't put a face on it.Then he started smelling a familiar scent. He started looking around trying to figure it out when his body got stiff. He felt as if a strong hand took the back of his head and pushed his head down so he was looking directly into his daughter's eyes. The familiar voice then said "this baby girl is god sent. She is God's way of blessing everything that has taken place in everyone's life the past few days. She is innocent and pure. She is a message from God. Do not corrupt her spirit for it is a godly one. She comes from great parents. She is a light from the creactor.Call her Amina.Take her out to her uncle and bring him in.He is still family. Show him that God is a forgiving God.

Before Blue had realized what he was doing he had started down the middle aisle and made his way through all the mourners' Q-Dog his partner was right behind them. As they got outside the crowd opened up for them to go in the direction of the patrol car Ahmad was in.When they got about fifteen feet away from the car the white detective got out with his hands on his gun shouting. Don't come any closer, he shouted at Blue. The black detective got out and stopped his partner, telling him everything was alright. He then rolled down Ahmad's window. Holding his daughter and as Ahmad looked up at them, all Blue could say was "her name is Amina".

The spirit was so strong the white detective opened Ahmads' door and without a word Ahmad got out and the six of them started in the church. Blue, baby Amina, Ahmad, Q-Dog, and the two detectives walked in and sat down in the front by the caskets alongside Ms. Dixon. There was not a dry eye in the church. When it was time to view the bodies, Blue couldn't move. He was too stiff to move. That's when the voice came back again and said," it's o.k. I understand". That's when it hit him. The voice he heard was Sharells'. The scent he smelt was her favorite perfume Rose. He had been visited by Sharells' spirit and it was very pleasing to him. Then the spirit said Te Amo Ppopi.Blue returned with I love you too baby.

The spirit of God works through life and death. Baby Amina has a path that is already paved for her by her creator to travel. She has already started her mission.

“HE THAT DWELLETH IN THE SECRET PLACE OF THE MOST HIGH SHALL ABIDE UNDER THE SHADOW OF THE ALMIGHTY. I WILL SAY OF THE LORD, HE IS MY REFUGE AND MY FORTRESS: MY GOD; IN HIM WILL I TRUST.” - PSALM 91:1-2

Chapter 6

CELEBRATION

Sitting on the fire escape of his apt. was one of Blues favorite spots to unwind and meditate. Only this time Blue was sitting there reminiscing. It was this very spot where he and Sharell shared their quality time together.
Blue was very happy with the big change that started happening in his community. Instead of liquor stores on each corner of the intersection of his block there was only one. On one corner now was a record store. On the other corner was a well needed grocery store. There was work being done on the last one. Some sort of community group was moving there. Even the movement on the block had changed. There were less negative spirits out there now. All of the drug dealers, pimps, prostitutes and drug users have moved on to other locations. Blue had written a poem on the hood right before Sharell had passed away. It went like this.

“The sounds of the night is a medley of organized chaos.The notes of this night symphony is lurking about, ready to cling on weak ears.

Got that rock, soft, girl, boy.Hey Poppi want a date tonight?

A language acknowledged only by those of us that danced to that beat.

A sound that caresses the soul of a once strong king or queen.

Weakened from the intoxicants of mortal man experimenting with gods people.

Dancing to the beat of the devil himself.

All off key, out of tune, no rhythm at all.

But some of us has danced to that beat.

But wait all of us has heard the majestic sound.

The composer of life

The one writer that holds the greatest title of all.

The beneficent, the merciful, master of the day of judgment.

But when we summit and dance to his tune he will assure us

the rhythm is always tight

He's always on beat

and most importantly soothing to the ears.

Let's listen to his music.

Let's dance to his beat.

If we surrender to his song

Stay focused

and practice his steps

We will waltz our way right into a productive life."

So looking at the hood now, he was thankful for the vast improvements .As he continued looking out at the street he was thankful for Rainbows gang members still holding down their promise of making a change. They were a big vessel in the major change. When these ex- gang members started patrolling the hood within one week everyone could see a major difference.

Today was an important day for blue. it was his clean from drugs date Anniversary. It was time for a celebration.Tonight was celebration night. Blue was in deep concentration because his celebration will be held at the same church that Sharell and Rainbows funeral was at. In fact that was the last time he had entered that church. For the past couple of years Blues celebrations had been very stressful .He would suffer head and anxiety attacks. This was the time of year that the loss of his wife would resurface and affect his emotions. This year Ms. Dixon and April took care of all the arrangements.

Ms. Dixon and April put together a beautiful celebration that was to start at 7:00 pm. It will be held at the Hilton hotel. They had it all worked out.all blue had to do was show up and that was no problem. They had a royal blue stretch limo pick Blue and Amina up at the house. Instead of the red carpet they had a royal blue carpet rolled out from the street to the hotel entrance. Once inside blue was amazed at how they had hooked up the ballroom with all royal blue decorations. Blue was escorted to his seat by Q-Dogs mother Sandra. Blue took his place and was giving a program of the evening's events.

As all the other guests were piling in they all came to

Blues table, congratulating him with hugs and kisses. April was the mistress of ceremonies. Attention everyone please take a seat we're about to start the celebration April announced.

This celebration was like no other. It started off with an inspiration award presentation. Up first was the group from Rainbows gang. They were now known as the "Loyal to the Street Crew". They all had on tee shirts with Sharell and Rainbows pictures on the front with the writings of "No matter What" in big letters. On the back in writing was "Loyal to the Streets Crew" .The president was Rainbow's first officer Left Eye.

Peace Bro. Blue, family and friends. They call me Left Eye. We are sincerely grateful to announce that we truly appreciate you for being an inspiration to Rainbow our brother. He spoke very highly of you and shared your dream of educating ourselves and our community. For that we are thankful. We are representing in the spirit of Rainbow and your dream in our community. We are happy to announce the we have started a new community foundation. It is well over due.it is called Rainbow Sharell Foundation. In both of their memories. Our community has donated over one hundred thousand dollars for the foundation and are asking that you sit on the board of directors. We are currently building a community center and it will be located in the last vacant storefront on your corner that used to be a liquor store. We pray that you accept our invitation and we congratulate you on the clean time you have been blessed with from the creator.Thank you.

Blue was happy to accept the invitation. He was even

more pleased that the creator put him in position to become an instrument in the rebuilding of a falling community. Blue received many more awards like that during the night .It was more of an appreciation night than a celebration night. Blue didn't mind because all he kept saying was "Praise and Thanks belongs to the Creator". When blue thought the evening couldn't get any better, April instructed everyone to focus on the silhouette to the right. Behind the screen was a tall man that stood about 6'2" tall. He had a slim build. When he started talking he had a very deep voice.

"Peace bro. Blue. I pray that this ceremony finds you and your family in the best of health and spirits. Congratulations on all of your clean time. Get more big brother". Blue was trying to put a face to the voice but he couldn't do it as the man continued. I must thank you for all you have done for me and my family. You are certainly an inspiration to me. I only wish that I connected with your godly spirit years ago. I do realize that the creator's time is the best of all timing and for that I am still grateful. Before I introduce this next speaker I'd like to share with you an emotional experience I have gone through. When first asked to be a speaker, here at your celebration I refused. I was concerned about what people may say or think. So I voiced my concern to this next speaker and they told me that God ,Sharell and Rainbow would want me here. I pray that you forgive me for the pain I have caused you and your family in the past. This next speaker reminded me that we serve a forgiving God. With that I am proud to introduce to you my niece and your daughter. A shining light of our creator, Amina.

This is when the ceremony took a real spiritual turn. Accompanied with the man from behind the curtain, Amina and her uncle Ahmad started walking toward Blue. It was so quiet that you could hear a pin drop in a pile of fluffy cotton. They started walking down the center aisle. Blue was happy to see his daughter being a part of his celebration but he couldn't tell how he was going to react to Ahmad being there .The closer they got, Ahmad was taking more and more form. He was much more muscular when he came from behind the curtain. He had dreadlocks that fell down to his waist but they were well kept. All kinds of things started going through Blues mind. Images of him raising Amina without her mother. Trying to hold both his family and the Dixon family together after the tragedy.The closer they got to him Blue was trying to figure out the last time he and Ahmad were face to face. It's been ten years or so, he thought. He didn’t know that Ahmad had even gotten out of jail. That walk down the aisle took an eternity for both Ahmad and Blue. As they got about ten feet from his table, Blue stood up. Finally they were all standing face to face.Ahmad was looking into Blues eyes. This was the vessel that was the author of the confusion that killed his wife, Blue thought. Blue started looking into Ahmad's spirit. That’s when Blue saw that Ahmad’s spirit had changed. He saw a man with principles’, a man with morals. A man that was sincerely trying to make amends. Without any words spoken Blue opened up his arms and gave Ahmad the biggest hug imaginable.Everyone stood up and exploded in a thunderous applause. It was not for blue to express himself.

Blue took the stage and thanked God for all that he had given him. The good and the bad. That’s when someone yelled out how many? Blues response was sixteen years. How did you do it was the next question. I have always had a guardian angel with me throughout my clean time that was sent to me by my creator. With tears in his eyes he directed everyone to the monitor to their right. I introduce to you second only to my God. My guardian angel, my wife Sharell. With the help of the 12 step world committee, Amina, now 15 years old and Blue put together a 20 minute slideshow of Sharell touching many lives all over the world. The slide was equipped with interviews from many people covering many nations. In the closing of the slide show Blue had gotten the hospital video of Sharells' last moments. The time when she had her family and the crew around her hospital bed. When she made them promise that "no matter what" they would not use drugs. They all said the serenity prayer and Sharell passed on with that spiritual smile on her face. Amina being only minutes old.

It was very hard for blue to maintain his emotions . Amina, noticing her father struggling, also with tears in her eyes went to the mic and did the closing. Daddy everyone here wanted to say something to you. When Blue looked up he saw the entire place on their feet most of them in tears yell in one big voice “no matter what”!!Blue couldn’t hold it in any longer and burst into a heavy cry.Amina hugged her father and whispered in his ear Te Amo Poppi. Blue whispered back. I Love You Too Baby.

to be continued.......

SAY: O MY SERVANTS WHO BELIEVE; KEEP YOUR DUTY TO YOUR LORD.FOR THOSE WHO DO GOOD IN THIS WORLD IS GOOD, AND ALLAH'S (GODS) EARTH IS SPACIOUS.TRULY THE STEADFAST WILL BE PAID THEIR REWARD WITHOUT MEASURE. QURAN SURA 39:10

About the Author

All praises are Due to Almighty God to whom I call Allah... Without him I would be nothing .With Him I know that there is nothing that I could do as long as he wishes it to be....Thanks Allah

Born to parents Charles and Dorothy Forrest under the name Charles Kevin Forrest. A true native of New York City. Living the Blessed life from a hard working father and a very supportive mother Charles took on a very unique personality. A very good student while in school Charles along with many peers grabbed a hold to the street as many of our youth do. At an early age of 14 Charles got into the music industry. Not letting go of the streets Charles romanced drugs, crime and violence. A combination that led to a 26 year drug addiction. While in the music business Charles change his name after finding Islam to Carlito Kalonji Muhammad. Carlito got married and started a wonderful family, moving away from the streets of New York to the south. Carlito was known as a dynamic D.J. working with groups such as Public Enemy, Biz Markie, Run D-M-C, KRS 1, and a host of other original Hip- Hop Giants.

In 1999 Carlito moved to Atlanta GA., expanded his experience, and formed Majestic Soundz, (later renamed Khalfani Radio International Health and Wealth) a music consultant company. This company also included artist management, artist development, and business management. `Majestic Soundz has also been blessed to place clients in major movies. "Fighting Temptations" with Beyoncé of

Destiny's Child, "Bring it On" with Gabrielle Union and "ATL" starring rap artist TI, are just a few.
Concerts are no stranger to Majestic Soundz, having put artists on tour as opening act for B2K, BOW-WOW, MONICA, and PUFF DADDY just to name a few.
Majestic Soundz has put together a team of well seasoned personnel dedicated to help artist that has what it takes to not only get to the top of their game but to stay on top of their game by way of the Majestic Soundz Marketing Team.

All of these Blessings however were one by one taken away from Carlito. All but his physical life was taken away. That is why Carlito is so grateful to the Almighty for every day of life…. Giving Him One More Chance to Get it Right!!!!…..

Since then Carlitos' road on recovery has been a little bumpy but he's grateful to be back on the road. Now he has taken his story to many places giving seminars ,helping the youth in trouble , and the ever growing Homeless problems around the world…

Gratitude and Thanks

All Praises Due to the Creator of Life…. Whom I call Allah….

I want to apologize to anyone that I may miss in my Thanks….

Thank you Mom and Dad, without the both of you my foundation would not have been strong enough to make it back to the right path of life after I had stepped off. Thanks to my sister Kim for her continued help and support for our parents when I was never available. To my brother Laz , thanks for being by my side through whatever I was going through. Thanks to The Hon. Min . Louis Farrakhan and The Nation of Islam for strengthening the Knowledge ,Wisdom and Understanding that was planted inside me from my mother and father. Thanks to St. Jude and M.s Donna for helping me through a difficult time in my life…26 years of sniffing Heroin.

A special Thanks To my Beautiful Wife UmmAbdulKarim and our Children Tonya,Leslie,Justine, Fatima, Shola and Bilal all Gifts from God…Poppi Loves You. My heart and thanks to the following persons…. Jason at Jefferson Place for helping me stay focused, Stephanie for the on job training to have a strong relationship, Lyvon madd love to you and the girls, Jameelah for her outstanding patience with me and love of Allah. Much thanks to **AZTANTA** and Celeste for believing me and helping me to reach a vision. Thank you Pastor Sherman for all of the truth that came from your spirit. Thanks to my Cuz Toni for keeping me in the loop when my mind started to go astray .To all my peeps in Central Islip Long Island and 40 Projects Queens NY….. Much Love and Thanks…, To the old crew…. Arnie Arn Swan ,Linda
R.I.P,Paulie,Tony,Darue,Roy,Cedric,Hector,Celeste,Stevie, Ronald,Taliesha,Illiana,Big E, Carl , Norman, Sonya , Tanya R.I.P, Sleep….
Special Thanks to you Leslie ,Some things Don't Have to be said to be Understood….. Much Love
Last be not least and because I am protected by Allah I want to thank Allah for Satan. I thank Allah for allowing me to go through the fire of the streets, drugs, crime violence, lies… and come out of it to be able to testify that

GOD IS ALWAYS VICTORIOUS

Authors Outro....

Dear Brothers and Sisters,

The easiest and perhaps the only way to facilitate change is by
allowing yourself to be influenced by a higher level of consciousness.
Think about it... Isn't this what you end up doing every single day?
One thought after another is trying to influence you every single
day.. A inspiring thought within you can banish fear inside of you
only if you allow it to ... A feel good energy within you can replace
doubt and anxiety within you only if you allow it to...
Try to change your current circumstances right now this moment...
You will struggle.. Why.?.. Because you are attempting to bring about

a radical change in your current circumstances using the power of your own thinking.... The fact is our current thinking represents our current circumstances and it cannot help us to achieve our goals and dreams... This is the biggest problem.. You break your head... you work hard you put in all efforts and nothing happens.. The reason is very simple ... It is not our fault... We have not understood the law of change....

The Greatest Law of change is simply "Uplift our level of Consciousness and EVERYTHING will fall into Place.

FinalCall.com) - Editor's note: The following article is based on a message delivered by Minister Farrakhan on December 11, 2004 to the Bloods and the Crips in Newark, New Jersey. This message is not only relevant to the Bloods and Crips, but also to all of the Black and Latino street organizations throughout the cities of America.

In The Name of Allah, The Beneficent, The Merciful.

Above all today, I am honored to be in the presence of my young Brothers, the Bloods and the Crips. I am very grateful to the leadership and those who follow that leadership who have tried their best to produce peace in the streets of Newark, New Jersey. There are too many mothers and grandmothers grieving because, in the natural sequence of things, parents should die before their children, having built a platform for them to stand on.

But circumstances in America and the world are such that children are dying before their mothers and grandmothers. Seeing a mother in a funeral parlor, grieving over her son who was shot down through the violence in the streets; feeling the pain of these mothers, fathers, grandmothers and grandfathers, gives way to great joy, knowing that you are making the effort to bring peace to the streets that you now control, to a degree.

***

Some of you were stopped by police on your way here, harassed for nothing but the fact that you are organized. An unwritten law among the slave-masters of our fathers and among the children of the slave-masters today is that Black people must never be allowed to organize. That frightens the government. Whenever there are Bloods, Crips, Black Gangster Disciples, El Rukns, or the Nation of Islam, the Black Panther Party or anybody that sees the value of coming together as an organized unit, you become dangerous.

Brothers, the best greeting that we could give is "peace." I offer you peace and you offered me peace in return, meaning that from my lips and hands, you have nothing to fear, because peace is what I have in my heart for you, and I hope you have peace in your heart for me. So, we offer each other peace.

The Honorable Minister Louis Farrakhan *Photos: Kenneth Muhammad*

Although you made a peace treaty, you need to understand the depth of what peace means. Peace means that I love for you what I love for myself. Peace means that I'll never go behind your back and talk about you, but if there's something in me that I want to say to you, I will talk directly to you, Brother to Brother, man to man, Sister to Sister. Backbiting breaks peace; slander breaks peace; gossip and rumors break peace.

The moment you made peace, some people were not happy. The people who should have been happy about your peace were very disturbed about it. Why should people in government become disturbed that you made peace in the street? The police should have been the first to say, "This is good. It makes our job easier." Instead of certain members of the police and city administration becoming happy about your peace, they immediately tried to break the peace.

We have become tribes and clans. Crip is a tribe. Blood is a tribe. Baptist is a tribe. Methodist is a tribe. Catholic is a tribe. Sunni Muslim is a tribe. Ahmadiya Muslim is a tribe. Nation of Islam is a tribe. As long as we think like tribes, the enemy—who put Shoshani against Navajo, against Hopi, against Cree—can keep you fighting each other, until a leader comes along who makes you able to see each other as one people and not a tribe. Whoever has the wisdom to break down the barriers that separate us from each other becomes the most dangerous individual to the aim of White people, which is to dominate the people of color of our planet.

When we practice peace, there has to be certain laws that we follow in order to bring peace. I cannot steal from you, yet offer you peace. I cannot come in your house, after your sister and desecrate your family, yet offer you peace. I cannot know that you are married and want your wife, yet offer you peace. I cannot sell drugs to destroy your household, yet offer you peace. If we mean peace—because there is too much hypocrisy around the word "peace"—then what supports our peace has to be the principle, "I treat you like I want you to treat me." This is a code of righteous conduct. Peace with a righteous code supporting it produces love.

The Crips and the Bloods, if you do not love each other, then you will not feel the pain of your Brother when he is hurt. When you hear that a Crip was shot, or a Blood was shot, why does it send shockwaves through all the Bloods of that group or set, or all the Crips of that set? You tell yourself, "We must take revenge because we feel the pain of the hurt of one of our members." But instead of Bloods feeling the pain of only Bloods, or Crips feeling the pain of only Crips, suppose Crips feel the pain of Bloods and Bloods feel the pain of Crips. Then, you would know that we are becoming a family now—a real family.

***

It is similar to our bodies. If someone steps on your toe, your toe does not speak, it is your mouth that opens in pain, because there is a connection between your mouth and your toe through a nervous system. The enemy does not want a replication of a nervous system developed among us, as a people, that when one of us aches, all of us feel that pain.

When we are connected like that, we will stop the enemy's evil treatment of us all over the country. You will not have to ask him to stop police brutality, we will stop it ourselves when we feel each others' pain.

But now, if somebody can kill our Christian family and we, as Muslims, do not feel their pain, then we are disconnected. If somebody can hang one of our Brothers in Georgia and we read about it in Newark, but do not feel the pain, then we are not tied to each other. In the '60s, we could not watch television in Newark and see dogs and firehoses aimed at Black people in Alabama and Mississippi, and not feel the pain. That's why when Martin Luther King, Jr. was shot down, 100 cities were set on fire because of rioting in the streets.

***

You may not realize that part of the strategy of the government is to put you all against each other. If the enemy sees you trying to organize, he will send people to organize you. He says, "You have a spirit to come together, but I am going to make sure that whoever leads you is my man." This is the way the enemy thinks. He always sets up a counterweight or a countermovement.

Fifteen years ago, when the Berlin Wall was torn down because East and West Germany decided to be one Germany, many of the CIA operatives working in Eastern Europe were brought back to the United States and assigned to gangs.

What was the aim of the government? Why do you think the only industry thriving today is the industry of prisons? Why do you think prisons are now on the stock market? People are investing in the prospect of Blacks and Latinos filling the jails.

Do you know that in the 13th Amendment, which says that slavery is abolished, there is a clause that many do not mention, that states, “except that when you are charged with a crime.” They are locking up our Brothers and Sisters all over the country, and when you are incarcerated, you lose your citizenship. This is a clever plan of the enemy. The Latino family is growing, so if Black gangs get tired of fighting each other, the enemy will produce another fight for you. They urge you on, saying “The Latinos are growing in power and you have to do something about that.” So, all of a sudden now, you find Black Brothers fighting their Latino Brothers. You all are being played against each other to somebody else’s benefit. When the police stopped you today, they asked each other if they had a warrant on any of you. You call it harassment, but it is also another means of placing leaders behind bars, where they can make a punk out of you.

When some of you are sent to prison, you begin to engage in sex with other men. When you come out of jail, you start living on the “down low”—you are in a relationship with a woman by day, and another man by night. You claim to be a heterosexual, while living a secret gay lifestyle. Most of our women who contract HIV/AIDS were infected with the virus during a heterosexual relationship with a man. And now, Black women are dying from AIDS more than any other group. Can you not see that the enemy is plotting our destruction and we are playing into his hands by destroying one another?

The government wants you killing each other because it makes its job easier. In every major city in America, and even minor cities, who is filling up the funeral parlors? It is our young Brothers age 18 to 35, either killed by AIDS, gunshot wounds, drug overdose or suicide. This is happening all over the country, Brothers, and it is part of a plot to deprive you of your future.

What is your future that the enemy knows, but you do not know? Do you think that you were born to be nothing, to walk the streets, smoke dope, have sex, party, dance, rap and die? Do you think that is what Allah (God) intends for you, the children of slaves who have suffered the worst slavery of any people in the annals of history? What kind of God would want that for you?

In the Bible, God tells Abraham, "Know of a surety that your seed, your offspring will be a stranger in a strange land and they are going to be afflicted in that land for 400 years. But after that time, I will come, and I will judge that nation which they shall serve, and afterward shall they come out with great substance and go to their father in peace and be buried in a good old age"—not buried as a young man. Then, Moses is raised as a prophet from among the Children of Israel, who are suffering in bondage for 400 years. Allah (God) plagues Pharaoh and his people, takes the Children of Israel out of the country. He gives them a land of their own—not a piece of sky, but people were on the land who looked like giants to the Children of Israel. Allah (God) told the Children of Israel, "Go in and take the land." But out of fear of facing the giants, their fathers said to God, Moses and Aaron, "You go in the land first and clean the giants out, then we will go." So God said to the elders, "I am going to let you wander in the wilderness until you die out. Then, I will take your children and they will inhabit the Promised

Land."

Later in the Bible, in the Book of Deuteronomy, there is a prophecy, where God says He will raise the seed of Abraham who will be in a strange land among strange people, and He will also raise them up a prophet like unto Moses. But you do not need a man like Moses unless you have a wicked king like Pharaoh and a people in bondage like the Children of Israel. Once God raises that man like Moses, He says, "I will put My words in his mouth and he will speak unto them, all that I shall command him." You may think this prophecy is referring to the Jews, but it is referring to Black people in America. Our fathers were brought to these shores 450 years ago, and this is a strange land and we have been like strangers in it and afflicted ever since we have been here.

Now, America sees the Judgment of God on her. Throughout the countries of the world, dislike is increasing for America. Anti-American sentiments are so bad now that they give travel advisories to Americans: "Don't go here. Don't go there." Americans even find it difficult to go to London, because the euro and the British pound weighs more than the American dollar. So, if you go to London, you have to spend a lot of money for little things that are much cheaper in America. The American dollar used to dominate the world economy, and if someone paid us, we would betray each other out of greed for money. I am warning those of you who think money is God, the wise economists are predicting that the dollar is going to collapse. After the dollar collapses, the government will collapse, as the Honorable Elijah Muhammad told me. Those who think that they have security in a dollar bill, rather than in God and the unity of their people, will cause blood to run in the streets.

The same bloodshed that is happening to the Palestinians by the Israelis will happen in America. The Palestinians have AK-47s, but the Israelis have helicopter gunships and jet planes flying over the Gaza Strip and the West Bank, firing rockets and killing Palestinian leaders. You have guns. Who do you think is giving you guns and why are they supplying you with guns? I am not your enemy, I only want to make you wise to what is about to happen. The enemy will send people to join the gangs in order to spread rumors about your Brother to cause you to fight and kill one another. These demons will even kill a policeman and then blame it on the gangs. You need to wake up and realize that you are dealing with a people with a mindset that is opposed to the thinking of God. You are not dealing with righteous people. The White man has not changed his treatment of us. A few of them will speak nice words to us but, in the end, we have not gained anything substantial as a people. Instead, we continue to live in hell, while the rich enjoy heaven at the poor's expense.

The enemy joins the gangs, like he did most of the Black organizations, and places snitches around our leaders. They pretend like they are a Crip or a Blood, but really they are agents of the government of the United States of America. They give you an AK-47, a MAC 10 and other weapons that are rejects and cannot shoot straight. So when you try to kill your Brother, a baby or somebody else innocent is killed instead as a result of your foolishness.

You are the people of God and God has come to take the bottom rail and bring it to the top, and make the last the first, and the least the most. But you are standing in the way of your own progress by your hatred of yourself and one another.

We, Muslims in the Nation of Islam, are not strangers to what you are facing on the streets. We are your Brothers, only we have been brought out of certain negative lifestyles with the Teachings of the Honorable Elijah Muhammad. We were killers, pimps, hustlers, robbers, thieves and liars, but we are reformed now. But we still share the same spirit of Brotherhood. The Honorable Elijah Muhammad said, "My greatest followers are still in the street." You are the best generation that we have ever produced. You are stronger than the generation we had in the '60s, you only need guidance.

***

Why can't these young people find something to do other than street life? When city governments set their budgets, why do they cut these young people out? Somebody has to speak up for them. How are White policemen able to harass them in a city that may be predominantly Black? Why can't they become the policemen who patrol and protect their communities? Are they going to be told, "You've been to jail so you cannot patrol your community?" Time is out for playing games. If Black leaders call it like it is, the enemy will back up, but if they are too afraid to open their mouths to speak for the voiceless poor, they need to get out of their offices and jobs.

***

I am hurting for these young people because I see their beauty and I see how they are being betrayed. The only people that can deceive you are the people that you trust. We are living in a time of betrayal. How did Yasser Arafat get poisoned? How did Yuaschenko of the Ukraine get poisoned? How did Indira Ghandi get killed? It is always someone close. How did Jesus get betrayed? There was a Judas in the family. You must understand that, during the height of the political movements of the '60s, the enemy had agents among us, pretending to be Muslims in the Nation of Islam, Socialists, Panthers, and even Christians in the church. They would say "Hallelujah" and "Praise the Lord" louder than everyone else, but they would also be reporting.

I am not trying to make you suspicious of one another, but I am trying to make you alert, because traps are being laid for the peacemakers. How can we mobilize the city for the 10th Anniversary of the Million Man March—which saw members of rival gangs embrace as Brothers—until we bring some peace to the streets? You cannot ask the Brothers to put their guns down if you do not have anything for them to do in return. You cannot give them lip service. Brothers have children; Brothers need jobs and income.

That's why I am concerned about these city budgets. Why can't city governments set aside money to train these Brothers in building skills? There are many run-down, dilapidated properties. If these Brothers were partnered with licensed plumbers, electricians, brick masons and painters, so that they could learn the skill, they could rehab and fix up these old abandoned houses. After the city sells the rehab buildings, they could put the profits in a Crip or Blood treasury, in order to buy more houses and land to start building their communities. When you start building, you control the streets but, right now, you do not own any part of the streets that you control. What good is controlling a street if you do not own it? You have to own it, then you are justified in controlling what you own. Then, when you own it, you want it run right.

Then, the next stage in community development is a Crip and a Blood getting elected to the city council. I heard that one of the Brothers told a city councilman, “We decide whose sign goes up, whose sign goes down in the streets that we control.” But suppose it’s your picture going up? Suppose you vote your man into office, and when your man is in, he has to represent the people who do not have any representation? And if those people on the city council refuse to divide the budget fairly, vote them out of the council and elect somebody who has your concern at heart.Then, look at the budget for the city’s schools. You may think that I am getting carried away, but I do not want to see my Brothers lose the promise of God.

They are the leaders of today and tomorrow, but they must be protected so they can grow into the manifestation of their powers.

A Special Thanks to my Brother Dwayne Muhammad

As I went through the cleansing of my mind body and soul from the addiction of Heroin I thank Brother Dwayne for displaying the True Meaning of Brotherly Love. Brother Dwayne never once looked down on me for my short comings. He always had an encouraging word for me during those dark times. He made sure that my family was well taken care of when I was absent from the house receiving the help that I needed. I will ALWAYS miss you Dwayne.

If you followed him on Twitter, you saw this tweet every morning around 7 a.m. from Dwayne Muhammad:

"IF YOU CAN READ THIS, GIVE GOD THANKS, BECAUSE SOME PEOPLE DIDN'T WAKE UP THIS MORNING. I'M THANKFUL, WHAT ABOUT YOU?"

On Sunday morning Dec 4th 2011, he did not send out the blessing. Bro Dwayne Muhammad, who founded the Pittsburgh Hip-Hop Awards in 2007, died from a sudden heart attack on Saturday at age 40 in Baltimore, where he was preparing for the South Jersey Hip-Hop Awards. A Pittsburgh native, Dwayne Muhammad formed the concert promotion company 360 Entertainment and promoted hip-hop concerts and events throughout the region. Inspired by the BET Hip Hop Awards show in Atlanta, he launched his own Pittsburgh Hip-Hop Awards in Pittsburgh in a big way, bringing in Mele Mel from Rock and Roll Hall of Fame group Grandmaster Flash and the Furious Five as emcee and honoring the unsung pioneers of the city's rap scene. From there, he launched similar events in such places as Harrisburg, Orlando and New Jersey and even helped organize a show in Nigeria.

My name is Charles Muhammad aka "Carlito". Because of our close relationship I have vowed not to let my brother Dwayne Muhammads vision go in vain.It's because of The Most High

& his example of true brotherhood is the reason why I survived that dark time in my life and resurrected the spirit within to produce what I have today.A message to ALL imitators out there it's time for the Original owner to take back his throne!!!Thank you Bro Dwayne Muhammad for your spirit.WE Love you,Miss you & this is in Memory of you!!

A Tribute to Bro Dwayne Muhammad and the Launching of the Dwayne Muhammad Hip Hop Awards Tour coming soon to your city.

www.ingramcontent.com/pod-product-compliance
Ingram Content Group UK Ltd.
Pitfield, Milton Keynes, MK11 3LW, UK
UKHW040558210726
13854UKWH00008B/1491